Christmas 2006

D.J. Chocolate
Wow! Chocolate
Grandma is going to
Love this Book

Much Love

Grandpa Grandma Jolie

& Aunt Natalie -
Alexandra & Gabrielle

xxoo xoxo

Dear D.J.,

have a great
christmas and
enjoy this book.

Love always,
Gabrielle
Luciano

CAKES
and Bakes

CAKES
and Bakes

p

This is a Parragon Publishing Book
First published in 2006

Parragon Publishing
Queen Street House
4 Queen Street
Bath BA1 1HE
United Kingdom

This edition designed by Fiona Roberts
Recipes and photography by The Bridgewater Book Company Ltd.

ISBN: 1-40547-231-6

Printed in Thailand

This book uses imperial, metric, or US cup measurements. Follow the same units of
measurement throughout; do not mix metric and imperial. All spoon measurements are
level: teaspoons are assumed to be 5 ml and tablespoons are assumed to be 15 ml.
Unless otherwise stated, milk is assumed to be whole, eggs and individual vegetables
such as potatoes are medium and pepper is freshly ground black pepper.

The times given for each recipe are an approximate guide only because the preparation
times may differ accordingly to the techniques used by different people and the cooking
times may vary as a result of the type of oven and other equipment used.

Recipes using raw or very lightly cooked eggs should be avoided by infants, the elderly,
pregnant women, convalescents and anyone suffering from an illness. Pregnant and
breastfeeding women are advised to avoid eating peanuts and peanut products.

CONTENTS

Time for some home-baking...

There is something special about home-baked cakes. It's not just that they are really delicious, nor even that they are delightfully different from those you can buy in the supermarket. It's more that they always seem like a delectable treat—and this is as true of a batch of easy-to-make muffins as it is of a richly decorated chocolate layer cake. Homemade cakes and slices turn any occasion into a special one, whether served at a fund-raising coffee morning, an old-fashioned afternoon tea party, or as a luxurious dessert at the end of a celebratory meal. They also make great after-school snacks and any-time-of-day nibbles when you need a pick-me-up.

There are several basic techniques, all of which are easy to master. These include creaming, rubbing-in, melting, and whisking and individual recipes provide clear instructions in the method. However, there are a few tips that are worth noting.

creaming: Fat and sugar are creamed together, that is beaten with a wooden spoon or an electric mixer, until the mixture is light and fluffy and has incorporated plenty of air. Butter produces a richer flavor than margarine, although either can be used. Sweet butter is best for cakes and other sweet baking. Superfine sugar is usually used as it is finer than granulated, but the type will always be specified in the recipe. When the fat and sugar are completely combined and aerated, the eggs are added. To avoid curdling, that is the mixture separating, eggs should always be beaten in gradually. If the mixture does begin to curdle, beat in a tablespoonful of flour before adding any more egg. Finally, the dry ingredients, such as flour, baking powder, and unsweetened cocoa powder, are folded in. Use a metal spoon or rubber spatula and gently stir in the flour using a figure-eight movement in order to avoid knocking out the air. Add the dry ingredients gradually and always sift them first.

rubbing-in: Fat is incorporated into the dry ingredients by rubbing it in with the fingertips or working it in with a pastry blender. The flour and other fine ingredients should be sifted into the bowl first and the fat—butter or margarine—is added. Cut it into the flour so that it is in small pieces, then rub in with the fingertips only, lifting the mixture high up in the bowl to incorporate air. Sugar may be stirred into the mixture before the fat is rubbed in but it is more usual to add it afterward, just before incorporating the liquid—commonly eggs or milk. Knead lightly to make sure that everything is thoroughly incorporated but try to avoid handling the mixture too much.

melting: Melted fat is beaten into sifted dry ingredients until the mixture is fully combined. This is a particularly easy method. Sift the dry ingredients into a bowl and set aside. Cut the fat—usually butter or margarine—into pieces and gently heat it in a small pan with any other specified ingredients, such as syrup, molasses or, sometimes, sugar, until melted and blended. Be careful not to overheat. Then either beat in the dry ingredients or beat the melted mixture into the dry ingredients according to the recipe.

whisking: In this method it is the eggs that are whisked. These may be whole or separated—the recipe will specify. Once plenty of air has been incorporated, dry ingredients, such as flour, cornstarch, and baking powder, should be gently folded in (see creaming opposite). There is no additional fat and cakes made by this method are very light.

top tips

✻ Don't substitute low-fat spreads for butter or margarine as their high water content makes them unsuitable for baking.
✻ Never measure liquid flavorings, such as almond extract, directly over the mixing bowl as it is easy to pour too much into the spoon which then splashes into the cake batter. Take similar care when adding food coloring.
✻ Always use the size and shape of cake pan specified in the recipe and grease and/or line it as described. Sweet butter is best for greasing as it is less likely to burn.
✻ Always preheat the oven to the required temperature and resist the temptation to open the oven door frequently. When checking the cake, open the oven door gently and only slightly, as a sudden draft is likely to make it "fall."
✻ Test a cake for "doneness" by pressing the top lightly with your fingertip. If the cake springs back immediately, it is ready. If your finger leaves a small dent, it requires further cooking. Alternatively, insert a wooden toothpick into the center of the cake. If it comes out clean, the cake is ready.

family favorites

Sponge Layer Cake

easy

serves 8 – 10

prep: 25 minutes +
cooling

25 – 30 minutes cooking

³/₄ cup sweet butter, softened, plus extra for greasing
scant 1 cup superfine sugar
3 eggs, beaten
1¹/₂ cups self-rising flour
3 tbsp jelly or lemon curd and 1 tbsp superfine or
confectioners' sugar, to serve

Preheat the oven to 350°F/180°C. Grease 2 x 8-inch/20-cm sponge cake pans with a little butter and line the bases with baking parchment.

Put the butter and superfine sugar in a mixing bowl and cream together until the mixture is pale, light, and fluffy. Cream for 1–2 minutes if using a hand-held mixer, or 5–6 minutes by hand. Add the eggs, a little at a time, beating well after each addition.

Sift the flour and carefully add it to the mixture, folding it in with a metal spoon or a spatula.

Divide the mixture between the two prepared layer pans and smooth over with the spatula. Bake on the same shelf in the center of the preheated oven for 25–30 minutes until well risen, golden brown, and beginning to shrink from the sides of the pans. Remove from the oven and let stand for 1 minute. Use a spatula to loosen the cakes from the edge of the pans.

Turn the cakes out onto a clean dish towel and remove the papers. Invert the cakes onto a cooling tray (this prevents the cooling tray from marking the top of the cakes). Leave for 30–45 minutes in a cool place to cool completely. Sandwich together with jelly or lemon curd, and sprinkle with the sugar.

Carrot Cake

Preheat the oven to 375°F/190°C. Grease a 9-inch/23-cm square cake pan with a little butter and line with baking parchment. In a mixing bowl, beat the eggs until well blended and add the sugar and oil. Mix well. Add the grated carrot.

Sift in the flour, baking soda, and spices, then add the walnuts. Mix everything together until well incorporated.

Spread the mixture into the prepared cake pan and bake in the center of the preheated oven for 40–50 minutes until the cake is nicely risen, firm to the touch, and has begun to shrink away slightly from the edge of the pan.

Remove from the oven and let cool in the pan until just warm, then turn out onto a cooling rack.

To make the topping, put all the ingredients into a mixing bowl and beat together for 2–3 minutes until really smooth.

When the cake is completely cold, spread with the topping, smooth over with a fork, and leave to firm up a little before cutting into 16 portions. Store in an airtight container in a cool place for up to 1 week.

easy

makes 16 pieces

prep: 30 minutes

40 – 50 minutes cooking

2 eggs
$^3/_4$ cup molasses sugar
scant 1 cup sunflower oil
generous 1 $^1/_3$ cups coarsely grated carrots
2 cups whole-wheat flour
1 tsp baking soda
2 tsp ground cinnamon
whole nutmeg, grated (about 1 tsp)
1 cup roughly chopped walnuts

TOPPING
$^1/_2$ cup half-fat cream cheese
4 tbsp butter, softened
$^3/_4$ cup confectioners' sugar
1 tsp grated lemon rind
1 tsp grated orange rind

Caraway Madeira

easy

serves 8

prep: 25 minutes +
cooling

1 hour cooking

1 cup butter, softened,
plus extra for greasing
scant 1 cup brown sugar
3 eggs, beaten lightly
2^1/$_2$ cups self-rising flour
1 tbsp caraway seeds
grated rind of 1 lemon
6 tbsp milk
1 or 2 strips of citron peel

Preheat the oven to 325°F/160°C. Grease a 2-lb/900-g loaf pan and line with baking parchment.

Cream the butter and brown sugar together in a bowl until pale and fluffy. Gradually add the beaten eggs to the creamed mixture, beating well after each addition. Sift the flour into the bowl and gently fold into the creamed mixture with a figure-eight movement.

Add the caraway seeds, lemon rind, and milk, and gently fold in until thoroughly blended. Spoon the mixture into the prepared pan and level the surface with a spatula. Bake in the preheated oven for 20 minutes.

Remove the cake from the oven and gently place the pieces of citron peel on top. Return to the oven and bake for 40 minutes more, or until the cake is well risen, golden, and a fine skewer inserted into the center comes out clean.

Let the cake cool in the pan for 10 minutes before turning out, then transfer it to a wire rack to let it cool completely.

Crunchy Fruit Cake

easy

serves 8

prep: 25 minutes +
cooling

1 hour cooking

$^1/_3$ cup butter, softened,
plus extra for greasing
$^1/_2$ cup superfine sugar
2 eggs, beaten lightly
generous $^1/_3$ cup self-rising
flour, sifted
1 tsp baking powder
$^2/_3$ cup cornmeal
1 $^1/_3$ cups mixed dried fruit
$^1/_4$ cup pine nuts
grated rind of 1 lemon
4 tbsp lemon juice
2 tbsp milk

Preheat the oven to 350°F/180°C. Grease a 7-inch/18-cm cake pan with a little butter and line the base with baking parchment.

Whisk the butter and sugar together in a bowl until light and fluffy. Whisk in the beaten eggs, a little at a time, whisking thoroughly after each addition. Gently fold the flour, baking powder, and cornmeal into the mixture until well blended. Stir in the mixed dried fruit, pine nuts, grated lemon rind, lemon juice, and milk.

Spoon the mixture into the pan and level the surface.

Bake in the preheated oven for about 1 hour, or until a fine metal skewer inserted into the center of the cake comes out clean.

Let the cake cool in the pan before turning out.

Apple Streusel Cake

easy

serves 8

prep: 20 minutes +
40 minutes cooling

1 hour cooking

¹/₂ cup butter, plus extra for greasing
1 lb/450 g tart cooking apples
1 ¹/₄ cups self-rising flour
1 tsp ground cinnamon
pinch of salt
generous ¹/₂ cup golden
superfine sugar
2 eggs
1–2 tbsp milk
confectioners' sugar, for dusting

STREUSEL TOPPING
generous ³/₄ cup self-rising flour
6 tbsp butter
scant ¹/₂ cup golden superfine sugar

Preheat the oven to 350°F/180°C, then grease a 9-inch/23-cm springform cake pan. To make the streusel topping, sift the flour into a bowl and rub in the butter until the mixture resembles coarse crumbs. Stir in the sugar and set aside.

Peel, core, and thinly slice the apples. To make the cake, sift the flour into a bowl with the cinnamon and salt. Place the butter and sugar in a separate bowl and beat together until light and fluffy. Gradually beat in the eggs, adding a little of the flour mixture with the last addition of egg. Gently fold in half the remaining flour mixture, then fold in the rest with the milk.

Spoon the batter into the prepared pan and smooth the top. Cover with the sliced apples and sprinkle the streusel topping evenly over the top. Bake in the preheated oven for 1 hour, or until browned and firm to the touch. Let cool in the pan before opening the sides. Dust the cake with confectioners' sugar before serving.

Cherry & Almond Cake

Preheat the oven to 325°F/160°C. Grease and line the bottom of a deep 7-inch/18-cm cake pan. Cut the cherries in half, then place them in a strainer and rinse to remove all the syrup. Pat dry with paper towels and set aside.

Place the butter, superfine sugar, eggs, and ground almonds in a bowl. Sift in the flour and baking powder. Beat thoroughly until smooth, then stir in the cherries. Spoon the batter into the prepared pan and smooth the top.

Sprinkle the slivered almonds over the cake. Bake in the preheated oven for $1^1/_2$–$1^3/_4$ hours, or until well risen and a skewer inserted into the center of the cake comes out clean. Let cool in the pan for 10 minutes, then turn out onto a wire rack, remove the lining paper, and let cool completely.

easy

serves 8

prep: 15 minutes +
30 minutes cooling

1 hour 30 minutes –
1 hour 45 minutes
cooking

$^3/_4$ cup butter, softened, plus extra for greasing
generous 1 cup candied cherries
scant 1 cup golden superfine sugar
3 eggs
$^2/_3$ cup ground almonds
generous 1$^1/_2$ cups all-purpose flour
1$^1/_2$ tsp baking powder
generous $^1/_3$ cup slivered almonds

Caribbean Coconut Cake

quite easy

serves 8

prep: 20 minutes +
30 minutes cooling

25 minutes cooking

1 1/4 cups butter, softened,
plus extra for greasing
scant 1 cup golden superfine sugar
3 eggs
1 1/4 cups self-rising flour
1 1/2 tsp baking powder
1/2 tsp freshly grated nutmeg
2/3 cup dry unsweetened coconut
5 tbsp coconut cream
2 3/4 cups confectioners' sugar
5 tbsp pineapple jelly

TO DECORATE
dry unsweetened coconut, toasted

Preheat the oven to 350°F/180°C. Grease and line the bottoms of 2 x 8-inch/20-cm sponge cake pans. Place 3/4 cup of the butter in a bowl with the sugar and eggs and sift in the flour, baking powder, and nutmeg. Beat together until smooth, then stir in the coconut and 2 tablespoons of the coconut cream.

Divide the mixture between the prepared pans and smooth the tops. Bake in the preheated oven for 25 minutes, or until golden and firm to the touch. Let cool in the pans for 5 minutes, then turn out onto a wire rack, peel off the lining paper, and let cool completely.

Sift the confectioners' sugar into a bowl and add the remaining butter and coconut cream. Beat together until smooth. Spread the pineapple jelly on one of the cakes and top with just under half of the buttercream. Place the other cake on top. Spread the remaining buttercream on top of the cake and scatter with the toasted coconut.

Pear & Ginger Cake

easy

serves 6

prep: 25 minutes +
cooking

40 minutes cooking

*scant 1 cup sweet butter,
softened, plus extra for greasing*
generous ³/₄ cup superfine sugar
1 ¹/₄ cups self-rising flour, sifted
1 tbsp ground ginger
3 eggs, beaten lightly
*1 lb/450 g pears, peeled, cored,
and thinly sliced, then brushed
with lemon juice*
1 tbsp brown sugar
*ice cream or heavy cream, lightly
whipped, to serve (optional)*

Preheat the oven to 350°F/180°C. Lightly grease a deep 8-inch/20-cm cake pan with butter and line the base with baking parchment. Mix all but 2 tablespoons of the butter with the superfine sugar, flour, ginger, and eggs in a bowl. Beat with a whisk until the mixture forms a smooth consistency.

Spoon the cake batter into the prepared pan and level out the surface with a spatula. Arrange the pear slices over the cake batter. Sprinkle with the brown sugar and dot with the remaining butter.

Bake in the preheated oven for 35–40 minutes, or until the cake is golden on top and feels springy to the touch.

Serve the pear and ginger cake warm, with ice cream or whipped cream, if you like.

Tuscan Christmas Cake

quite easy

serves 12 – 14

prep: 35 minutes +
cooling

1 hour cooking

generous $^3/_4$ cup hazelnuts
generous $^3/_4$ cup almonds
$^1/_2$ cup candied peel
$^1/_3$ cup dried apricots, chopped finely
$^1/_3$ cup candied pineapple, chopped finely
grated rind of 1 orange
scant $^1/_2$ cup all-purpose flour
2 tbsp unsweetened cocoa
1 tsp ground cinnamon
$^1/_4$ tsp ground coriander
$^1/_4$ tsp freshly grated nutmeg
$^1/_4$ tsp ground cloves
generous $^1/_2$ cup superfine sugar
$^1/_2$ cup honey

TO DECORATE
confectioners' sugar

Line an 8-inch/20-cm cake pan with parchment paper. Spread out the hazelnuts on a baking sheet and toast in a preheated oven, 350°F/180°C, for 10 minutes, until golden brown. Pour them onto a dish towel and rub off the skins. Meanwhile, spread out the almonds on a baking sheet and toast in the oven for 10 minutes, until golden. Watch carefully after 7 minutes because they can burn easily. Reduce the oven temperature to 300°F/150°C. Chop all the nuts and place in a large bowl.

Add the candied peel, apricots, pineapple, and orange rind to the nuts and mix well. Sift together the flour, unsweetened cocoa, cinnamon, coriander, nutmeg, and cloves into the bowl and mix well.

Put the sugar and honey into a pan and set over low heat, stirring, until the sugar has dissolved. Bring to a boil and cook for 5 minutes, until thickened and starting to darken. Stir the nut mixture into the pan and remove from the heat.

Spoon the mixture into the prepared cake pan and level the surface with the back of a damp spoon. Bake in the oven for 1 hour, then transfer to a wire rack to cool in the pan.

Carefully remove the cake from the pan and peel off the parchment paper. Just before serving, dredge the top with confectioners' sugar. Cut into thin wedges to serve.

Honey Spice Cake

Preheat the oven to 350°F/180°C. Grease a 3¹/₂-cup fluted cake pan. Place the butter, sugar, honey, and water into a heavy-bottom pan. Set over low heat and stir until the butter has melted and the sugar has dissolved. Remove from the heat and let cool for 10 minutes.

Sift the flour into a bowl and mix in the ginger, cinnamon, caraway seeds, and cardamom. Make a well in the center. Pour in the honey mixture and the eggs and beat well until smooth. Pour the batter into the prepared pan and bake in the preheated oven for 40–50 minutes, or until well risen and a skewer inserted into the center comes out clean. Let cool in the pan for 5 minutes, then transfer to a wire rack to cool completely.

Sift the confectioners' sugar into a bowl. Stir in enough warm water to make a smooth, flowing frosting. Spoon over the cake, allowing it to flow down the sides, then let set.

easy

serves 8

prep: 15 minutes +
30 minutes cooling

40 – 50 minutes
cooking

²/₃ cup butter, plus extra for greasing
generous ¹/₂ cup brown sugar
¹/₂ cup honey
1 tbsp water
scant 1¹/₂ cups self-rising flour
¹/₂ tsp ground ginger
¹/₂ tsp ground cinnamon
¹/₂ tsp caraway seeds
seeds from 8 cardamom pods, ground
2 eggs, beaten
3¹/₂ cups confectioners' sugar

Date & Walnut Teabread

easy

serves 10

prep: 20 minutes +
20 minutes cooling

1 hour – 1 hour 15 minutes
cooking

³/₄ cup butter, plus extra
for greasing
scant 1¹/₃ cups pitted dates,
chopped into small pieces
grated rind and juice of 1 orange
scant ¹/₄ cup water
scant 1 cup brown sugar
3 eggs, beaten
²/₃ cup whole-wheat
self-rising flour
²/₃ cup white self-rising flour
¹/₃ cup chopped walnuts
8 walnut halves

TO DECORATE

orange zest

Preheat the oven to 325°F/160°C. Grease and line the bottom and ends of a 2-lb/900-g loaf pan. Place the dates in a pan with the orange rind and juice and water and cook over medium heat for 5 minutes, stirring, or until it is a soft purée.

Place the butter and sugar in a bowl and beat together until light and fluffy. Gradually beat in the eggs, then sift in the flours and fold in with the chopped walnuts. Spread one-third of the mixture over the bottom of the prepared loaf pan and spread half the date purée over the top.

Repeat the layers, ending with the cake mixture. Arrange walnut halves on top. Bake in the oven for 1–1¹/₄ hours, or until well risen and firm to the touch. Let cool in the pan for 10 minutes. Turn out, peel off the lining paper, and transfer to a wire rack to cool. Decorate with orange zest and serve in slices.

Banana & Cranberry Loaf

easy

serves 10

prep: 20 minutes

1 hour cooking

1 tbsp butter, for greasing
1 ¹/₄ cups self-rising flour
¹/₂ tsp baking powder
³/₄ cup brown sugar
2 bananas, mashed
¹/₃ cup chopped candied peel
2 tbsp chopped mixed nuts
¹/₄ cup dried cranberries
5–6 tbsp orange juice
2 eggs, beaten lightly
²/₃ cup sunflower oil
³/₄ cup confectioners' sugar, sifted
grated rind of 1 orange

Preheat the oven to 350°F/180°C. Grease a 2-lb/900-g loaf pan with the butter and line the base with baking parchment.

Sift the flour and baking powder into a mixing bowl. Stir in the sugar, bananas, chopped candied peel, nuts, and cranberries.

Stir the orange juice, eggs, and oil together, until thoroughly blended. Add the mixture to the dry ingredients and mix well. Pour the mixture into the prepared pan and level the surface with a spatula.

Bake in the preheated oven for about 1 hour, until firm to the touch or until a fine metal skewer inserted into the center of the loaf comes out clean. Turn out the loaf onto a wire rack and let cool completely.

Mix the confectioners' sugar with a little water and drizzle the frosting over the loaf. Sprinkle orange rind over the top. Let the frosting set before serving the loaf in slices.

Marbled Chocolate & Orange Teabread

quite easy

serves 12

prep: 20 minutes +
20 minutes cooling

35 – 40 minutes cooking

²/₃ cup butter, softened, plus extra for greasing
2³/₄ oz/75 g semisweet chocolate, broken into pieces
1¹/₄ cups golden superfine sugar
5 large eggs, beaten
generous 1 cup all-purpose flour
2 tsp baking powder
pinch of salt
grated rind of 2 oranges

Preheat the oven to 350°F/180°C. Grease and line the bottom and ends of 2 x 1-lb/450-g loaf pans. Place the chocolate in a bowl set over a pan of simmering water, making sure that the bottom of the bowl does not touch the water. Remove from the heat once the chocolate has melted.

Place the butter and sugar in a separate bowl and beat until light and fluffy. Gradually beat in the eggs. Sift the flour, baking powder, and salt into the mixture and fold in.

Transfer one-third of the mixture to the melted chocolate and stir. Stir the orange rind into the remaining mixture and spread one-fourth of the mixture evenly in each cake pan. Drop spoonfuls of the chocolate mixture on top, dividing it between the 2 pans, but do not smooth it out. Divide the remaining orange mixture between the 2 pans, then, using a knife, gently swirl the top 2 layers together to give a marbled effect.

Bake in the preheated oven for 35–40 minutes, or until a skewer inserted into the center comes out clean. Let cool in the pans for 10 minutes, then turn out, peel off the lining paper, and transfer to a wire rack to cool completely.

Sticky Ginger Marmalade Loaf

easy

serves 10

prep: 10 minutes +
10 minutes cooling

1 hour cooking

³/4 cup butter, softened,
plus extra for greasing
¹/3 cup ginger marmalade
scant 1 cup brown sugar
3 eggs, beaten
generous 1 ¹/2 cups self-rising flour
¹/2 tsp baking powder
1 tsp ground ginger
²/3 cup coarsely chopped pecans

Preheat the oven to 350°F/180°C. Grease and line the bottom and ends of a 2-lb/900-g loaf pan. Place 1 tablespoon of the ginger marmalade in a small pan and reserve. Place the remaining marmalade in a bowl with the butter, sugar, and eggs.

Sift in the flour, baking powder, and ground ginger and beat together until smooth. Stir in three-quarters of the nuts. Spoon the mixture into the prepared loaf pan and smooth the top. Sprinkle with the remaining nuts and bake in the preheated oven for 1 hour, or until well risen and a skewer inserted into the center comes out clean.

Let cool in the pan for 10 minutes, then turn out and peel off the lining paper. Transfer to a wire rack to cool until warm. Set the pan of reserved marmalade over low heat to warm, then brush over the loaf and serve in slices.

Sticky Date Cake

quite easy

serves 8

prep: 20 minutes +
30 minutes cooling

1 hour – 1 hour 15 minutes
cooking

scant 1 ^{1}/$_3$ cups pitted dates,
chopped
1 ^{1}/$_4$ cups boiling water
^{1}/$_2$ cup butter, softened,
plus extra for greasing
scant 1 cup golden superfine sugar
3 eggs, beaten
generous 1 ^{1}/$_2$ cups self-rising
flour, sifted
^{1}/$_2$ tsp ground cinnamon
1 tsp baking soda

TOPPING

scant ^{1}/$_2$ cup brown sugar
4 tbsp butter
3 tbsp heavy cream

Place the dates in a bowl and cover them with the boiling water. Preheat the oven to 350°F/180°C, then grease a 9-inch/23-cm springform cake pan. Place the butter and sugar in a bowl and beat until light and fluffy. Gradually beat in the eggs, then fold in the flour and cinnamon.

Add the baking soda to the dates and water, then pour onto the creamed mixture. Stir until well mixed. Pour into the prepared pan and bake in the oven for 1–1^1/$_4$ hours, or until well risen and firm to the touch.

Preheat the broiler to medium. To make the topping, place the sugar, butter, and cream in a pan. Set over low heat, stirring, until the sugar has melted, then bring to a boil and let simmer for 3 minutes. Pour over the cake and place the cake under the preheated broiler until the topping is bubbling. Let cool in the pan until the topping has set, then transfer to a wire rack to cool completely before serving.

Banana & Lime Cake

easy

serves 10

prep: 35 minutes +
45 minutes cooling

40 - 45 minutes cooking

butter, for greasing
scant 2 cups all-purpose flour
1 tsp salt
1 1/2 tsp baking powder
scant 7/8 cup firmly packed brown sugar
1 tsp grated lime rind
1 egg, beaten
1 banana, mashed with 1 tbsp
lime juice
2/3 cup lowfat mascarpone cheese
2/3 cup golden raisins

TOPPING

1 cup confectioners' sugar
1–2 tsp lime juice
1/2 tsp finely grated lime rind

TO DECORATE

banana chips
finely grated lime rind

Preheat the oven to 350°F/180°C. Grease and line a deep 7-inch/18-cm round cake pan with parchment paper. Sift the flour, salt, and baking powder into a large bowl and stir in the sugar and lime rind.

Make a well in the center of the dry ingredients and add the egg, banana, mascarpone cheese, and golden raisins. Mix well until thoroughly incorporated. Spoon the batter into the pan and smooth the surface.

Bake in the preheated oven for 40–45 minutes, or until firm to the touch or until a skewer inserted in the center comes out clean. Let the cake cool in the pan for 10 minutes, then turn out onto a wire rack to cool completely.

To make the topping, sift the confectioners' sugar into a small bowl and mix with the lime juice to form a soft, but not too runny frosting. Stir in the grated lime rind. Drizzle the frosting over the cake, letting it run down the sides. Decorate the cake with banana chips and lime rind. Let the cake stand for 15 minutes so that the frosting sets.

slices & traybakes

Scottish Petticoat Tails Shortbread

very easy

makes 8

prep: 20 minutes + cooling

45 – 50 minutes cooking

¹/₂ cup butter, cut into small pieces, plus extra for greasing
scant 1 ¹/₂ cup all-purpose flour, plus 1 tbsp for dusting
pinch of salt
4 tbsp superfine sugar
2 tsp golden superfine sugar

Preheat the oven to 300°F/150°C. Grease an 8-inch/20-cm fluted shallow baking pan.

Mix together the flour, salt, and sugar. Rub the butter into the dry ingredients. Continue to work the mixture until it forms a soft dough. Make sure you do not overwork the shortbread or it will be tough, not crumbly as it should be.

Lightly press the dough into the cake pan. If you don't have a fluted or plain shallow cake pan, roll out the dough on a lightly floured board, place on a baking sheet and pinch the edges to form a scalloped pattern.

Mark into 8 pieces with a knife. Prick all over with a fork and bake in the center of the oven for 45-50 minutes until the shortbread is firm and just colored.

Allow to cool in the pan and dust with the sugar. Cut into portions and remove to a wire rack. Store in an airtight container in a cool place until needed.

Ginger-Topped Fingers

Preheat the oven to 350°F/180°C. Grease an 11 x 7-inch/28 x 18-cm rectangular cake pan. Sift the flour and ginger into a bowl and stir in the sugar. Rub in the butter until the cookie dough starts to stick together.

Press the cookie dough into the prepared pan and smooth the top with a spatula. Bake in the preheated oven for 40 minutes, or until very lightly browned.

To make the topping, place the syrup and butter in a small pan over low heat and stir until melted. Stir in the confectioner's sugar and ginger. Remove the shortbread from the oven and pour the topping over it while both are still hot. Let cool slightly in the pan, then cut into 16 fingers. Transfer to wire racks to cool.

very easy

makes 16

prep: 15 minutes +
30 minutes cooling

40 minutes cooking

$^3/_4$ cup butter, plus extra for greasing
generous 1 $^1/_2$ cups all-purpose flour
1 tsp ground ginger
scant $^1/_2$ cup golden superfine sugar

GINGER TOPPING
1 tbsp corn syrup
$^1/_4$ cup butter
2 tbsp confectioners' sugar
1 tsp ground ginger

Cinammon & Seed Squares

very easy

makes 12

prep: 10 minutes,
plus 1 hour cooling

45 minutes cooking

generous 1 cup butter, softened,
plus extra for greasing
generous 1¹/₄ cups superfine sugar
3 eggs, beaten
generous 1⁵/₈ cups self-rising flour
¹/₂ tsp baking soda
1 tbsp ground cinnamon
²/₃ cup sour cream
scant ¹/₂ cup sunflower seeds

Preheat the oven to 350°F/180°C. Grease a 9-inch/23-cm square cake pan and line the bottom with parchment paper. Beat the butter and superfine sugar together in a large bowl until the batter is light and fluffy. Gradually add the beaten eggs to the batter, beating thoroughly after each addition.

Sift the self-rising flour, baking soda, and ground cinnamon into the creamed batter and fold in gently, using a metal spoon. Spoon in the sour cream and sunflower seeds and gently mix until well combined.

Spoon the batter into the prepared cake pan and smooth the surface with the back of a spoon or a knife. Bake in the preheated oven for 45 minutes, or until the mixture is firm to the touch when pressed with a finger.

Loosen the edges with a round-bladed knife, then turn out onto a wire rack to cool completely. Slice into 12 squares.

Almond Slices

easy

makes 8

prep: 15 minutes

45 minutes cooking

3 eggs
²/₃ cup ground almonds
1 ¹/₂ cups dry milk
1 cup granulated sugar
¹/₂ tsp saffron threads
scant ¹/₂ cup sweet butter
1 tbsp sliced almonds, to decorate

Preheat the oven to 325°F/160°C. Beat the eggs together in a bowl and set aside.

Place the ground almonds, dry milk, sugar, and saffron in a large mixing bowl and mix well.

Melt the butter in a small pan over low heat. Pour the melted butter over the dry ingredients and mix well until thoroughly blended. Add the reserved beaten eggs to the mixture and mix well.

Spread the cake mixture evenly in a shallow 7–9-inch/15–20-cm ovenproof dish and bake in the preheated oven for 45 minutes, or until a fine metal skewer inserted into the center of the cake comes out clean.

Cut the almond cake into 8 slices. Decorate the almond slices with sliced almonds, and transfer to serving plates. Serve hot or cold.

Chocolate Peppermint Slices

easy

makes 16

prep: 15 minutes

10 – 15 minutes cooking

4 tbsp butter, plus extra for greasing
¹/4 cup superfine sugar
³/4 cup all-purpose flour
2 cups confectioners' sugar
¹/2 tsp peppermint extract
6 oz/175 g semisweet chocolate,
broken into pieces
1–2 tbsp warm water

Preheat the oven to 350°F/180°C. Grease and line an 8 x 12-inch/ 20 x 30-cm jelly roll pan with parchment paper. Whisk the butter and sugar together until pale and fluffy. Stir in the flour until the mixture binds together.

Knead the mixture to form a smooth dough, then press into the prepared pan. Prick the surface all over with a fork. Bake the base in the preheated oven for 10–15 minutes, until lightly browned and just firm to the touch. Let cool in the pan.

Sift the confectioners' sugar into a bowl. Gradually add the water, then add the peppermint extract. Spread the frosting over the base, then let set.

Melt the chocolate in a heatproof bowl set over a pan of gently simmering water, then spread over the peppermint frosting. Let set, then cut into slices.

Chocolate Caramel Squares

Preheat the oven to 350°F/180°C. Beat together the margarine and brown sugar in a bowl until light and fluffy. Beat in the flour and the rolled oats. Use your fingertips to bring the mixture together, if necessary.

Press the mixture into the base of a shallow 8-inch/20-cm square cake pan.

Bake the cookies in the preheated oven for 25 minutes, or until just golden and firm. Cool in the pan.

Place the ingredients for the caramel filling in a saucepan and heat gently, stirring until the sugar has dissolved. Bring slowly to a boil over very low heat, then boil very gently for 3–4 minutes, stirring constantly, until thickened.

Pour the caramel filling over the oat layer in the pan and let set.

Melt the semisweet chocolate and spread it over the caramel. If using the white chocolate, place in a heatproof bowl set over a saucepan of gently simmering water until melted. Pipe lines of white chocolate over the semisweet chocolate. Using a toothpick, feather the white chocolate into the semisweet chocolate. Let set, then cut into squares to serve.

very easy

makes 16

prep: 40 minutes

25 minutes cooking

generous $^1/_3$ cup soft margarine
$^1/_3$ cup brown sugar
1 cup all-purpose flour
$^1/_2$ cup rolled oats

CARAMEL FILLING
2 tbsp butter
2 tbsp brown sugar
generous $^3/_4$ cup condensed milk

TOPPING
$3^1/_2$ oz/100 g semisweet chocolate
1 oz/25 g white chocolate (optional)

Coconut Oat Crunch Bars

very easy

makes 16

prep: 15 minutes +
30 minutes cooling

30 minutes cooking

scant 1 cup butter,
plus extra for greasing
1 cup raw brown sugar
2 tbsp corn syrup
3 cups rolled oats
scant $^3/_4$ cup dry
unsweetened coconut
$^1/_2$ cup candied cherries, chopped

Preheat the oven to 325°F/160°C, then grease a 12 x 9-inch/30 x 23-cm cookie sheet.

Heat the butter, sugar, and syrup in a large pan over low heat until just melted. Stir in the oats, coconut, and cherries and mix until evenly combined.

Spread the mixture evenly onto the cookie sheet and press down with the back of a spatula to form a smooth surface.

Bake in the preheated oven for 30 minutes. Remove from the oven and let cool on the cookie sheet for 10 minutes. Cut the crunch bars into rectangles using a sharp knife. Carefully transfer the bars to a wire rack and let cool completely.

Nutty Oat Squares

very easy

makes 16

prep: 10 minutes +
30 minutes cooling

20 - 25 minutes cooking

$^1/_2$ cup butter
plus extra for greasing
scant $2^3/_4$ cups rolled oats
$^3/_4$ cup chopped hazelnuts
6 tbsp all-purpose flour
2 tbsp corn syrup
scant $^1/_2$ cup brown sugar

Preheat the oven to 350°F/180°C, then grease a 9-inch/23-cm square ovenproof dish or cake pan. Place the rolled oats, chopped hazelnuts, and flour in a large mixing bowl and stir together.

Place the butter, syrup, and sugar in a pan over low heat and stir until melted. Pour onto the dry ingredients and mix well. Turn into the prepared ovenproof dish and smooth the surface with the back of a spoon.

Bake in the oven for 20–25 minutes, or until golden and firm to the touch. Mark into 16 pieces and let cool in the dish. When completely cold, cut through with a sharp knife and remove from the dish.

Chocolate Marshmallow Fingers

very easy

makes 18

prep: 10 minutes +
2 – 3 hours chilling

0 minutes cooking

12 oz/350 g graham crackers
4^1/$_2$ oz/125 g semisweet chocolate,
broken into pieces
1 cup butter
^{1}/$_8$ cup superfine sugar
2 tbsp unsweetened cocoa
2 tbsp honey
^{2}/$_3$ cup mini marshmallows
^{1}/$_2$ cup white chocolate chips

Put the graham crackers in a polythene bag and, using a rolling pin, crush into small pieces.

Put the chocolate, butter, sugar, cocoa, and honey in a pan and heat gently until melted. Remove from the heat and let cool slightly.

Stir the crushed crackers into the chocolate mixture until well mixed. Add the marshmallows and mix well then finally stir in the chocolate chips.

Turn the mixture into an 8-inch/20-cm square cake pan and lightly smooth the top. Put in the refrigerator and let chill for 2–3 hours, until set. Cut into fingers before serving.

Chocolate Slab Cake

Preheat the oven to 375°F/190°C. Grease a 13 x 8-inch/33 x 20-cm square cake pan and line the bottom with parchment paper. Melt the butter and chocolate with the water in a pan over low heat, stirring frequently.

Sift the flour and baking powder into a mixing bowl and stir in the sugar.

Pour the hot chocolate liquid into the bowl and then beat well until all of the ingredients are evenly mixed. Stir in the sour cream, followed by the eggs.

Pour the cake batter into the cake pan and bake in the preheated oven for 40–45 minutes, until springy to the touch.

Let the cake cool slightly in the pan before turning it out on to a wire rack. Let cool completely.

To make the frosting, melt the chocolate with the water in a pan over very low heat, stir in the cream and remove from the heat. Stir in the chilled butter, then pour the frosting over the cooled cake, using a spatula to spread it evenly over the top of the cake.

very easy

serves 4

prep: 55 minutes

40 – 45 minutes cooking

scant 1 cup butter, plus extra for greasing
3¹/₂ oz/100 g bittersweet chocolate, broken into pieces
¹/₃ cup water
2¹/₂ cups all-purpose flour
2 tsp baking powder
1¹/₃ cups brown sugar
¹/₃ cup sour cream
2 eggs, beaten

FROSTING

7 oz/200 g bittersweet chocolate
6 tbsp water
3 tbsp light cream
1 tbsp butter, chilled

Walnut & Cinnamon Blondies

easy

makes 9

prep: 10 minutes +
30 minutes cooling

20 – 25 minutes cooking

1 cup butter,
plus extra for greasing
generous 1 cup brown sugar
1 egg
1 egg yolk
1 cup self-rising flour
1 tsp ground cinnamon
generous $^1/_2$ cup coarsely
chopped walnuts

Preheat the oven to 350°F/180°C. Grease and line the bottom of a 7-inch/18-cm square cake pan. Place the butter and sugar in a pan over low heat and stir until the sugar has dissolved. Cook, stirring, for an additional 1 minute. The mixture will bubble slightly, but do not let it boil. Let cool for 10 minutes.

Stir the egg and egg yolk into the mixture. Sift in the flour and cinnamon, add the nuts, and stir until just blended. Pour the cake batter into the prepared pan, then bake in the preheated oven for 20–25 minutes, or until springy in the center and a skewer inserted into the center of the cake comes out clean.

Let cool in the pan for a few minutes, then run a knife round the edge of the cake to loosen it. Turn the cake out onto a wire rack and peel off the paper. Let cool completely. When cold, cut into squares.

Gingerbread

easy

makes 12

prep: 15 minutes

30 – 35 minutes cooking

^{2}/₃ cup butter,
plus extra for greasing
scant 1 cup brown sugar
2 tbsp molasses
generous 1 ^{1}/₂ cups
all-purpose flour
1 tsp baking powder
2 tsp baking soda
2 tsp ground ginger
^{2}/₃ cup milk
1 egg, beaten lightly
2 eating apples, peeled, chopped,
and coated with lemon juice

Preheat the oven to 325°F/160°C. Grease a 9-inch/23-cm square cake pan with a little butter and line with baking parchment.

Melt the butter, sugar, and molasses in a pan over low heat. Remove from the heat and let cool.

Sift the flour, baking powder, baking soda, and ground ginger together into a mixing bowl. Stir in the milk, egg, and cooled butter and molasses mixture, followed by the chopped apples. Stir gently, then pour the mixture into the prepared pan, and level the surface with a spatula.

Bake in the preheated oven for 30–35 minutes, until the cake has risen and a fine metal skewer inserted into the center comes out clean.

Let the ginger cake cool in the pan, then turn out, and cut into 12 bars.

chocolate treats

Chocolate Brownies

very easy

serves 4

prep: 20 minutes +
1 - 2 hours to cool/set

30 minutes cooking

1 cup butter, diced, plus extra for greasing
5¹/₂ oz/150 g dark chocolate, chopped
1¹/₂ cups all-purpose flour
1 cup dark muscovado sugar
4 eggs, beaten
¹/₄ cup blanched hazelnuts, chopped
¹/₂ cup golden raisins
¹/₂ cup dark chocolate chips

TO DECORATE
4 oz/115 g white chocolate, melted

Preheat the oven to 350°F/180°C. Grease and line an 11 x 7-inch/ 28 x 18-cm rectangular cake pan.

Put the butter and chopped dark chocolate into a heatproof bowl and set over a pan of simmering water until melted. Remove from the heat. Sift the flour into a large bowl, add the sugar, and mix well. Stir the eggs into the chocolate mixture, then beat into the flour mixture. Add the nuts, golden raisins, and chocolate chips and mix well. Spoon evenly into the cake pan and level the surface.

Bake in the oven for 30 minutes, or until firm. To check whether the cake is cooked through, insert a toothpick into the center—it should come out clean. If not, return the cake to the oven for a few minutes. Remove from the oven and let cool for 15 minutes. Turn out on to a wire rack to cool completely. To decorate, drizzle the melted white chocolate in fine lines over the cake, then cut into bars or squares. Let set before serving.

Ginger Chocolate Chip Squares

Preheat the oven to 300°F/150°C. Finely chop the preserved ginger. Sift the flour, ground ginger, cinnamon, cloves, and nutmeg into a large bowl. Stir in the chopped preserved ginger and sugar.

Put the butter and the syrup in a pan and heat gently until melted. Bring to a boil, then pour the mixture into the flour mixture, stirring all the time. Beat until the mixture is cool enough to handle.

Add the chocolate chips to the mixture. Press evenly into a 8 x 12-inch/ 20 x 30-cm jelly roll pan.

Bake in the oven for 30 minutes. Cut into squares, then let cool in the pan.

very easy

makes 15

prep: 10 minutes

30 minutes cooking

4 pieces preserved ginger in syrup

1 $^1/_2$ cups all-purpose flour

1 $^1/_2$ tsp ground ginger

1 tsp ground cinnamon

$^1/_4$ tsp ground cloves

$^1/_4$ tsp grated nutmeg

$^1/_2$ cup brown sugar

$^1/_2$ cup butter

$^1/_3$ cup corn syrup

$^1/_2$ cup semisweet chocolate chips

Chocolate Temptations

very easy

makes 24

prep: 15 – 20 minutes

16 minutes cooking

scant $^1/_2$ cup butter,
plus extra for greasing
12$^1/_2$ oz/365 g semisweet
chocolate
1 tsp strong coffee
2 eggs
scant $^3/_4$ cup brown sugar
generous 1$^1/_3$ cups all-purpose flour
$^1/_4$ tsp baking powder
pinch of salt
2 tsp almond extract
scant $^2/_3$ cup chopped Brazil nuts
scant $^2/_3$ cup chopped hazelnuts
1$^1/_2$ oz/40 g white chocolate

Preheat the oven to 350°F/180°C. Grease a large cookie sheet. Put 8 oz/225 g of the semisweet chocolate with the butter and the coffee into a heatproof bowl set over a pan of gently simmering water and heat until the chocolate is almost melted.

Meanwhile, beat the eggs in a bowl until fluffy. Whisk in the sugar gradually until thick. Remove the chocolate from the heat and stir until smooth. Add to the egg mixture and stir until combined.

Sift the flour, baking powder, and salt into a bowl and stir into the chocolate mixture. Chop 3 oz/85 g of semisweet chocolate into pieces and stir into the dough. Stir in the almond extract and nuts.

Put 24 tablespoonfuls of the dough on to the cookie sheet, transfer to the preheated oven and bake for 16 minutes. Transfer the cookies to a wire rack to cool. To decorate, melt the remaining chocolate (semisweet and white) in turn, then spoon into a pastry bag and pipe lines on to the cookies.

Chocolate Chip Cookies

very easy

serves 4

prep: 15 minutes +
cooling

12 – 15 minutes cooking

*generous ¹/₂ cup butter,
softened, plus extra for greasing*
1 cup dark muscovado sugar
1 egg, beaten
1¹/₂ cups self-rising flour
2 tbsp unsweetened cocoa powder
1 tsp almond extract
*4¹/₄ oz/120 g dark
chocolate chips*
¹/₂ cup chopped mixed nuts

Preheat the oven to 375°F/190°C. Grease two large cookie sheets.

Put the butter and sugar into a large bowl and cream until fluffy. Gradually beat in the egg. Sift the flour and cocoa powder into a separate bowl, then fold into the egg mixture with the almond extract. Stir in the chocolate chips and nuts. Drop rounded teaspoonfuls of the mixture on to the prepared cookie sheets, leaving plenty of space between them to allow them to spread during cooking.

Bake in the oven for 12–15 minutes, or until golden. Remove from the oven, transfer to wire racks, and let cool completely. Store in an airtight tin until ready to serve.

Double Chocolate Muffins

easy

makes 12

prep: 15 minutes + cooling

20 minutes cooking

scant 1 1/2 cups all-purpose flour
1/3 cup unsweetened cocoa,
plus extra for dusting
1 tbsp baking powder
1 tsp ground cinnamon
generous 1/2 cup golden
superfine sugar
6 1/2 oz/185 g white chocolate,
broken into pieces
2 large eggs
generous 1/3 cup sunflower-seed or peanut oil
1 cup milk

Preheat the oven to 400°F/200°C. Line a 12-cup muffin pan with muffin paper liners. Sift the flour, cocoa, baking powder, and cinnamon into a large mixing bowl. Stir in the sugar and 4 1/2 oz/125 g of the white chocolate.

Place the eggs and oil in a separate bowl and whisk until frothy, then gradually whisk in the milk. Stir into the dry ingredients until just blended. Divide the batter evenly between the paper liners, filling each three-quarters full. Bake in the oven for 20 minutes, or until well risen and springy to the touch. Remove the muffins from the oven, let cool in the pan for 2 minutes, then remove them and place them on a cooling rack to cool completely.

Place the remaining white chocolate in a heatproof bowl, set the bowl over a pan of barely simmering water, and heat until melted. Spread over the top of the muffins. Let set, then dust the tops with a little cocoa and serve.

Chocolate Pistachio Cookies

easy

makes 24

prep: 25 minutes +
30 minutes cooling

30 minutes cooking

2 tbsp butter, sweet for preference,
plus extra for greasing
6 oz/175 g semisweet chocolate,
broken into pieces
2¹/₂ cups self-rising flour,
plus extra for dusting
1¹/₂ tsp baking powder
scant ¹/₂ cup superfine sugar
¹/₂ cup cornmeal
finely grated rind of 1 lemon
2 tsp amaretto
1 egg, beaten lightly
³/₄ cup coarsely chopped
pistachios
2 tbsp confectioners sugar,
for dusting

Preheat the oven to 325°F/160°C. Grease a cookie sheet with butter. Put the chocolate and 2 tablespoons of butter in a heatproof bowl set over a pan of gently simmering water. Stir over low heat until melted and smooth. Remove from the heat and cool slightly.

Sift the flour and baking powder into a bowl and mix in the superfine sugar, cornmeal, lemon rind, amaretto, egg, and pistachios. Stir in the chocolate mixture and mix to a soft dough.

Lightly dust your hands with flour, divide the dough in half, and shape each piece into an 11-inch/28-cm long cylinder. Transfer the cylinders to the prepared cookie sheet and flatten, with the palm of your hand, to about ³/₄ inch/2 cm thick. Bake the cookies in the preheated oven for about 20 minutes, until firm to the touch.

Remove the cookie sheet from the oven and let the cooked pieces cool. When cool, put the cooked pieces on a cutting board and slice them diagonally into thin cookies. Return them to the cookie sheet and bake for an additional 10 minutes, until crisp. Remove from the oven, and transfer to a wire rack to cool. Dust lightly with confectioners' sugar.

White Chocolate Cake

easy

serves 4 – 6

prep: 30 minutes +
cooling/chilling overnight

20 minutes cooking

CAKE

butter, for greasing
4 eggs
generous $^1/_2$ cup superfine sugar
1 cup all-purpose flour, sifted
pinch of salt
1 $^1/_4$ cups heavy cream
5$^1/_2$ oz/150 g white chocolate, chopped

CHOCOLATE LEAVES

3 oz/90 g dark or
white chocolate, melted
handful of rose leaves, or
other small edible leaves with
well-defined veins, washed and dried

To make the leaves, brush the melted chocolate over the underside of the leaves. Arrange, coated sides up, on a cookie sheet lined with parchment paper. Chill until set, then peel away the leaves.

Preheat the oven to 350°F/180°C. Grease and line an 8-inch/20-cm round cake tin. Put the eggs and sugar into a heatproof bowl and set over a pan of barely simmering water. Whisk until thick, remove from the heat, and whisk until cool. Fold in the flour and salt. Pour into the pan and bake for 20 minutes, then cool for 10 minutes. Turn out, discard the lining paper, and let cool.

Put the cream into a pan over low heat and bring to a boil, stirring. Add the chocolate and stir until melted. Pour into a bowl, cover with plastic wrap, and chill overnight.

Cut the cake horizontally in half. Whisk the cream until thick, spread one-third over half of the cake and top with the other, then coat with the remaining cream. Chill for 1–2 hours, decorate with the chocolate leaves and serve.

Chocolate Cake with Syrup

very easy

serves 12

prep: 15 minutes

35 minutes cooking

$^1/_2$ cup sweet butter,
plus extra for greasing
8 oz/225 g semisweet chocolate,
broken into pieces
1 tbsp strong black coffee
4 large eggs
2 egg yolks
generous $^1/_2$ cup golden superfine sugar
generous $^1/_3$ cup all-purpose flour
2 tsp ground cinnamon
scant $^1/_2$ cup ground almonds

TO DECORATE

chocolate-covered coffee beans,

SYRUP

1 $^1/_4$ cups strong black coffee
generous $^1/_2$ cup golden superfine sugar
1 cinnamon stick

Preheat the oven to 375°F/190°C. Grease and base-line the bottom of a deep 8-inch/20-cm round cake pan. Place the chocolate, butter, and coffee in a heatproof bowl and set over a pan of gently simmering water until melted. Stir to blend, then remove from the heat and let cool slightly.

Place the whole eggs, egg yolks, and sugar in a separate bowl and whisk together until thick and pale. Sift the flour and cinnamon over the egg mixture. Add the almonds and the chocolate mixture and fold in carefully. Spoon the cake batter into the prepared pan. Bake in the preheated oven for 35 minutes, or until the tip of a knife inserted into the center comes out clean. Let cool slightly before turning out on to a serving plate.

Meanwhile, make the syrup. Place the coffee, sugar, and cinnamon stick in a heavy-based pan and heat gently, stirring, until the sugar has dissolved. Increase the heat and boil for 5 minutes, or until reduced and thickened slightly. Keep warm. Pierce the surface of the cake with a toothpick, then drizzle over half the coffee syrup. Decorate with chocolate-covered coffee beans and serve, cut into wedges, with the remaining coffee syrup.

Chocolate Fudge Gateau

Preheat the oven to 350°F/180°C. Lightly oil and line the base of 2 x 8-inch/20-cm shallow cake pans with nonstick baking paper. Melt the chocolate in a heatproof bowl set over a pan of gently simmering water. Cream the butter and sugar together until light and fluffy then gradually add the eggs, beating well between each addition and adding a little flour after each addition. When all the eggs have been added, stir in the melted chocolate and then the remaining flour and mix lightly together.

Stir in the ground almonds together with 1–2 tablespoons of cooled boiled water. Mix to form a soft dropping consistency. Stir in the fudge pieces then divide between the 2 lined cake pans and smooth the tops. Bake in the preheated oven for 35–40 minutes or until the tops spring back when touched lightly with a finger. Remove and let cool before turning out on to wire racks and discarding the lining paper. Leave until cold.

Beat the butter for the frosting until soft and creamy then gradually beat in the confectioners' sugar, adding a little cream as the mixture becomes stiff. Add the muscovado sugar together with the unsweetened cocoa and stir lightly. Stir in sufficient of the remaining cream to give a soft spreadable frosting.

Place the grated chocolate on a sheet of nonstick parchment paper. Split the cakes in half horizontally and sandwich together with a third of the prepared frosting. Spread another third around the sides then roll the cake in the grated chocolate. Place on a serving plate. Spread the top with the remaining frosting, piping rosettes around the outside edge for an attractive finish. Decorate with the truffles before serving.

easy

serves 10

prep: 20 minutes

35 – 40 minutes cooking

1 tsp sunflower oil, for oiling
3 oz/85 g semisweet chocolate
1 cup butter, softened
1 cup light muscovado sugar
4 eggs, beaten
1 $^1/_2$ cups self-rising flour
generous $^1/_2$ cup ground almonds
4 oz/115 g soft vanilla fudge,
chopped small

FROSTING
$^3/_4$ cup butter, softened
2$^1/_2$ cups confectioners' sugar, sifted
3–4 tbsp light cream
$^1/_4$ cup light muscovado sugar
1 tbsp unsweetened cocoa, sifted

TO DECORATE
2 oz/55 g semisweet chocolate, grated
cocoa-dusted truffles

Chocolate Banana Loaf

easy

serves 4 – 6

prep: 15 minutes

1 hour cooking

¹/₂ cup sweet butter, softened,
plus extra for greasing
1 ¹/₃ cups soft brown sugar
2 eggs
3 bananas
2 cups all-purpose flour
1 tsp bicarbonate of soda
1 tbsp unsweetened cocoa powder
1 tsp allspice
¹/₃ cup thick natural yogurt
3 oz/85 g semisweet chocolate chips

Preheat the oven to 350°F/180°C. Grease a 9 x 5 x 3-inch/23 x 13 x 7.5-cm loaf pan.

Put the butter, sugar, and eggs into a bowl and beat well. Peel and mash the bananas, then add to the mixture. Stir in well. Sift the flour, bicarbonate of soda, cocoa powder, and allspice into a separate bowl, then add to the banana mixture and mix well. Stir in the yogurt and chocolate chips. Spoon the mixture into the prepared pan and level the surface.

Bake in the oven for 1 hour. To test whether the loaf is cooked through, insert a tooth pick into the center—it should come out clean. If not, return the loaf to the oven for a few minutes.

Deep Chocolate Cheesecake

very easy

serves 4 – 6

prep: 15 - 20 minutes +
4 hours to chill

0 min cooking

BASE

*4 tbsp butter, melted,
plus extra for greasing
1 cup (about 14 squares)
finely crushed graham crackers
2 tbsp sugar
2 tsp unsweetened cocoa powder*

CHOCOLATE LAYER

*1 lb 12 oz/800 g
mascarpone cheese
1 1/2 cups confectioners' sugar, sifted
juice of 1/2 orange
finely grated rind of 1 orange
6 oz/175 g dark chocolate, melted
2 tbsp brandy*

TO DECORATE

*chocolate leaves (see page 65)
halved kumquats*

Grease an 8-inch/20-cm springform cake pan.

To make the base, put the crushed graham crackers, sugar, cocoa powder, and melted butter into a large bowl and mix well. Press the mixture evenly over the base of the prepared pan.

Put the mascarpone and sugar into a bowl and stir in the orange juice and rind. Add the melted chocolate and brandy, and mix together until thoroughly combined. Spread the chocolate mixture evenly over the crumb layer. Cover with plastic wrap and chill for at least 4 hours.

Remove the cheesecake from the refrigerator, turn out on to a serving platter and decorate with chocolate leaves and kumquat halves. Serve immediately.

Chocolate Cherry Gateau

easy

serves 8

prep: 15 minutes +
30 minutes to cool

40 minutes cooking

3 tbsp unsalted butter, melted, plus extra for greasing
2 lb/900 g fresh cherries, pitted and halved
generous 1 1/4 cups superfine sugar
scant 1/2 cup cherry brandy
3/4 cup all-purpose flour
1/2 cup unsweetened cocoa
1/2 tsp baking powder
4 eggs
4 cups heavy cream

TO DECORATE
grated semisweet chocolate
whole fresh cherries

Preheat the oven to 350°F/180°C. Grease and line a 9-inch/ 23-cm springform cake pan. Put the halved cherries into a pan, add 3 tablespoons of the sugar and the cherry brandy. Simmer for 5 minutes. Drain, reserving the syrup. In another bowl, sift together the flour, cocoa, and baking powder.

Put the eggs in a heatproof bowl and beat in a generous 3/4 cup of the sugar. Place the bowl over a pan of simmering water and beat for 6 minutes until thickened. Remove from the heat, then gradually fold in the flour mixture and melted butter. Spoon into the cake pan. Bake for 40 minutes. Remove from the oven and let cool.

Turn out the cake and cut in half horizontally. Mix the cream with the remaining sugar. Spread the reserved syrup over the cut sides of the cake. Arrange the cherries over one half, top with a layer of cream, and place the other half on top. Cover with cream, press grated chocolate all over, and decorate with cherries.

Chocolate Truffle Cake

Preheat the oven to 350°F/180°C. Lightly grease and base-line an 8-inch/20-cm round springform pan. Beat the butter and sugar together until light and fluffy. Gradually add the eggs, beating well after each addition.

Sift the flour, baking powder, and unsweetened cocoa together and fold into the cake batter along with the ground almonds. Pour into the prepared pan and bake in the preheated oven for 20–25 minutes, or until springy to the touch. Let the cake cool slightly in the pan, then transfer to a wire rack to cool completely. Wash and dry the pan and return the cooled cake to the pan.

To make the topping, heat the chocolate, butter, and cream in a heavy-based pan over low heat and stir until smooth. Cool, then chill for 30 minutes. Beat well with a wooden spoon and chill for an additional 30 minutes. Beat the mixture again, then add the cake crumbs and rum, beating until well combined. Spoon over the sponge cake and let chill for 3 hours.

Meanwhile, put the chocolate in a heatproof bowl set over a pan of gently simmering water until melted. Dip the cape gooseberries in the melted chocolate until partially covered. Let set on parchment paper. Transfer the cake to a serving plate; decorate with the cape gooseberries.

very easy

serves 12

prep: 45 minutes +
4 hours chilling

20 – 25 minutes cooking

¹/₃ cup butter plus extra for greasing
¹/₃ cup superfine sugar
2 eggs, beaten lightly
²/₃ cup self-rising flour
¹/₂ tsp baking powder
¹/₄ cup unsweetened cocoa
¹/₂ cup ground almonds

TRUFFLE TOPPING
12 oz/350 g semisweet chocolate
¹/₂ cup butter
1¹/₄ cups heavy cream
1¹/₄ cups plain cake crumbs
3 tbsp dark rum

TO DECORATE
1³/₄ oz/50 g semisweet chocolate, broken into pieces
cape gooseberries

small bites

Lavender Fairy Cakes

very easy

makes 12

prep: 15 minutes +
20 minutes cooling

12 – 15 minutes cooking

generous $^1/_2$ cup golden
superfine sugar
$^1/_2$ cup butter, softened
2 eggs, beaten
1 tbsp milk
1 tsp finely chopped
lavender flowers
$^1/_2$ tsp vanilla extract
1$^1/_4$ cups self-rising flour, sifted
scant 1$^1/_2$ cups confectioners'
sugar

TO DECORATE
lavender flowers
silver dragées

Preheat the oven to 400°F/200°C. Place 12 paper cake cases in a muffin pan. Place the superfine sugar and butter in a bowl and cream together until pale and fluffy. Gradually beat in the eggs. Stir in the milk, lavender, and vanilla extract, then carefully fold in the flour.

Divide the mixture between the paper cases and bake in the oven for 12–15 minutes, or until well risen and golden. The sponge should bounce back when pressed. A few minutes before the cakes are ready, sift the confectioners' sugar into a bowl and stir in enough water to make a thick frosting.

When the cakes are baked, transfer to a wire rack and place a blob of frosting in the center of each one, allowing it to run across the cake. Decorate with lavender flowers and silver dragées and serve as soon as the cakes are cool.

Chocolate Butterfly Cakes

easy

makes 12

prep: 30 minutes

15 minutes cooking

$^1/_2$ cup soft margarine
$^1/_2$ cup superfine sugar
1 $^1/_4$ cups self-rising flour
2 large eggs
2 tbsp unsweetened cocoa
1 oz/25 g semisweet
chocolate, melted
confectioners' sugar, for dusting

LEMON BUTTERCREAM

6 tbsp butter, sweet for
preference, softened
1 $^1/_3$ cups confectioners' sugar, sifted
grated rind of $^1/_2$ lemon
1 tbsp lemon juice

Preheat the oven to 350°F/180°C. Line a shallow muffin pan with 12 muffin paper cases. Place all of the ingredients for the cakes, except for the melted chocolate and confectioners' sugar, in a large bowl, and beat with an electric whisk until the mixture is just smooth. Beat in the melted chocolate.

Spoon equal amounts of the batter into each paper case, filling them three-quarters full. Bake in the preheated oven for 15 minutes, or until springy to the touch. Transfer to a wire rack and let cool.

Meanwhile, make the lemon buttercream. Place the butter in a mixing bowl and beat until fluffy, then gradually beat in the confectioners' sugar. Beat in the lemon rind and gradually add the lemon juice, beating well.

When cold, cut the top off each cake, using a serrated knife. Cut each cake top in half.

Spread or pipe the buttercream frosting over the cut surface of each cake and push the 2 cut pieces of cake top into the frosting to form wings. Dust with confectioners' sugar.

Chocolate Cup Cakes

easy

makes 18

prep: 20 minutes +
1 hour chilling

20 minutes cooking

6 tbsp butter, softened
$^1/_2$ cup superfine sugar
2 eggs, lightly beaten
2 tbsp milk
$^1/_3$ cup semisweet chocolate chips
1 $^1/_4$ cups self-rising flour
$^1/_4$ cup unsweetened cocoa

FROSTING
8 oz/225 g white chocolate
5$^1/_2$ oz/150 g lowfat cream cheese

Preheat the oven to 400°F/200°C. Line a shallow muffin pan with 18 muffin paper cases.

Beat together the butter and sugar until pale and fluffy. Gradually add the eggs, beating well after each addition. Add a little of the flour if the mixture starts to curdle. Add the milk, then fold in the chocolate chips.

Sift together the flour and cocoa and fold into the batter with a metal spoon or spatula. Divide the batter equally among the muffin paper cases and smooth the tops.

Bake in the preheated oven for 20 minutes, or until well risen and springy to the touch. Cool on a wire rack.

To make the frosting, melt the chocolate in a heatproof bowl set over a pan of gently simmering water. Cool slightly. Beat the cream cheese until softened, then beat in the chocolate. Spread a little of the frosting over each cake and let chill for 1 hour before serving.

Lowfat Blueberry Muffins

Preheat the oven to 375°F/190°C. Spray a 12-cup muffin pan with vegetable oil cooking spray, or line it with 12 muffin paper liners. Sift the flour, baking soda, salt, and half of the allspice into a large mixing bowl. Add 6 tablespoons of the superfine sugar and mix together.

In a separate bowl, whisk the egg whites together. Add the margarine, yogurt, and vanilla extract and mix together well, then stir in the fresh blueberries until thoroughly mixed. Add the fruit mixture to the flour mixture and then gently stir together until just combined. Do not overstir the batter—it is fine for it to be a little lumpy.

Divide the muffin batter evenly between the 12 cups in the muffin pan or the paper liners (they should be about two-thirds full). Mix the remaining sugar with the remaining allspice, then sprinkle the mixture over the muffins. Transfer to the oven and bake for 25 minutes, or until risen and golden. Remove the muffins from the oven and serve warm, or place them on a cooling rack and let cool.

very easy

makes 12

prep: 15 minutes + cooling

25 minutes cooking

vegetable oil cooking spray, for oiling (if using)
scant $1^5/8$ cups all-purpose flour
1 tsp baking soda
$^1/_4$ tsp salt
1 tsp allspice
generous $^1/_2$ cup superfine sugar
3 large egg whites
3 tbsp lowfat margarine
$^2/_3$ cup thick, lowfat, plain or blueberry-flavored yogurt
1 tsp vanilla extract
$^3/_4$ cup fresh blueberries

Fruity Muffins

very easy

makes 10

prep: 15 minutes +
cooling

25 – 30 minutes cooking

2 cups self-rising whole wheat flour
2 tsp baking powder
2 tbsp brown sugar
generous $^1/_2$ cup
no-soak dried apricots,
finely chopped
1 banana, mashed with
1 tbsp orange juice
1 tsp finely grated
orange rind
1$^1/_4$ cups skim milk
1 large egg, beaten
3 tbsp sunflower-seed or peanut oil
2 tbsp rolled oats
fruit spread, honey, or maple syrup,
to serve

Preheat the oven to 400°F/200°C. Line 10 cups of a 12-cup muffin pan with muffin paper liners. Sift the flour and baking powder into a mixing bowl, adding any husks that remain in the strainer. Stir in the sugar and chopped apricots.

Make a well in the center and add the mashed banana, orange rind, milk, beaten egg, and oil. Mix together well to form a thick batter and divide evenly between the muffin liners.

Sprinkle with a few rolled oats and bake in the oven for 25–30 minutes until well risen and firm to the touch, or until a toothpick inserted into the center comes out clean.

Remove the muffins from the oven and place them on a cooling rack to cool slightly. Serve the muffins while still warm with a little fruit spread, honey, or maple syrup.

Cranberry Muffins

very easy

makes 18

prep : 15 minutes +
cooling

20 minutes cooking

butter, for greasing
generous 1 $^1/_2$ cups
all-purpose flour
2 tsp baking powder
$^1/_2$ tsp salt
$^1/_4$ cup superfine sugar
4 tbsp butter, melted
2 large eggs, lightly beaten
$^3/_4$ cup milk
1 $^1/_8$ cups fresh cranberries
$^1/_4$ cup freshly grated
Parmesan cheese

Preheat the oven to 400°F/200°C. Lightly grease 2 x 9-cup muffin pans with butter.

Sift the flour, baking powder, and salt into a mixing bowl. Stir in the superfine sugar.

In a separate bowl, combine the butter, beaten eggs, and milk, then pour into the bowl of dry ingredients. Mix lightly together until all of the ingredients are evenly combined, then stir in the fresh cranberries.

Divide the batter evenly between the prepared 18 cups in the muffin pans. Sprinkle the grated Parmesan cheese over the top.

Transfer to the oven and bake for 20 minutes, or until the muffins are well risen and a golden brown color.

Remove the muffins from the oven and let them cool slightly in the pans. Place the muffins on a cooling rack and let cool completely.

Biscuits

easy

makes 16

prep: 20 minutes

10 – 12 minutes cooking

3^1/$_2$ cups all-purpose flour
^{1}/$_2$ tsp salt
2 tsp baking soda
4 tbsp butter
2 tbsp superfine sugar
1 cup milk
3 tbsp milk, for glazing
strawberry conserve and whipped heavy cream, to serve

Preheat the oven to 425°F/220°C.

Sift the flour, salt, and baking soda into a bowl. Rub in the butter until the mixture resembles bread crumbs. Stir in the sugar.

Make a well in the center and pour in the milk. Stir in using a palette knife and make a soft dough.

Turn the mixture onto a floured surface and lightly flatten the dough until it is of an even thickness, about ^{1}/$_2$ inch. Don't be heavy-handed, biscuits need a light touch.

Use a 2^1/$_2$-inch/6-cm cookie cutter to cut out the scones and place on the baking sheet. Glaze with a little milk and bake for 10-12 minutes, until golden and well risen.

Cool on a wire rack and serve freshly baked with strawberry conserve and whipped heavy cream.

Oaty Pecan Cookies

Preheat the oven to 350°F/180°C, then grease 2 cookie sheets. Place the butter and sugar in a bowl and beat until light and fluffy. Gradually beat in the egg, then stir in the nuts.

Sift the flour and baking powder into the mixture and add the oats. Stir together until well combined. Drop spoonfuls of the mixture on to the prepared cookie sheets, spaced well apart to allow for spreading.

Bake in the oven for 15 minutes, or until pale golden. Let cool on the cookie sheets for 2 minutes, then transfer to wire racks to cool completely.

very easy

makes 15

prep: 10 minutes +
20 minutes cooling

15 minutes cooking

$^1/_2$ cup butter, softened, plus extra for greasing
scant $^1/_2$ cup brown sugar
1 egg, beaten
$^1/_3$ cup chopped pecans
$^2/_3$ cup all-purpose flour
$^1/_2$ tsp baking powder
$^2/_3$ cup rolled oats

Rock Drops

very easy

makes 8

prep: 15 minutes + cooling

15 – 20 minutes cooking

$^1/_3$ cup butter,
diced, plus extra for greasing
scant 1$^1/_2$ cups all-purpose flour
2 tsp baking powder
$^1/_3$ cup raw brown sugar
$^1/_2$ cup golden raisins
2 tbsp candied cherries,
chopped finely
1 egg, beaten lightly
2 tbsp milk

Preheat oven to 400°F/200°C. Lightly grease a cookie sheet with a little butter.

Sift the flour and baking powder into a mixing bowl. Rub in the butter with your fingertips until the mixture resembles bread crumbs. Stir in the raw brown sugar, raisins, and candied cherries. Add the beaten egg and milk to the mixture and bring together to form a soft dough.

Spoon 8 mounds of the mixture onto the prepared cookie sheet, spacing them well apart to allow room to expand during cooking. Bake in the preheated oven for 15–20 minutes, until firm to the touch when pressed with a finger.

Remove the rock drops from the cookie sheet. Serve piping hot from the oven, or transfer to a wire rack and let cool before serving.

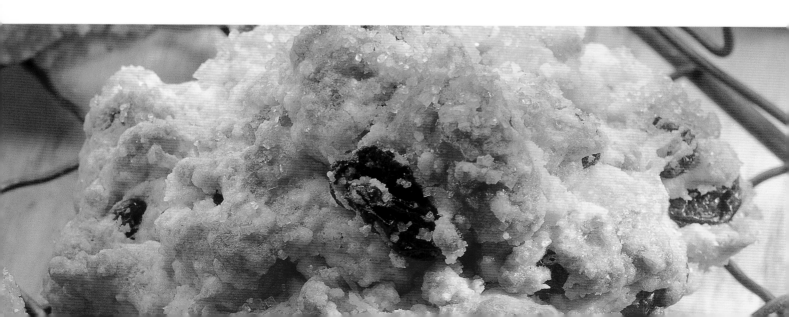

Orange & Walnut Cakes

easy

makes 18

prep: 20 minutes +
cooling

20 minutes cooking

3 cups self-rising flour
¹/₂ tsp baking soda
¹/₂ tsp ground cinnamon
¹/₄ tsp ground cloves
pinch of grated nutmeg
pinch of salt
1 *¹/₄* cups olive oil
¹/₃ cup superfine sugar
finely grated rind and
juice of 1 large orange

TOPPING
¹/₄ cup walnut pieces,
chopped finely
¹/₂ tsp ground cinnamon

SYRUP
¹/₂ cup Greek honey
¹/₂ cup water
juice of 1 small lemon
juice of 1 small orange or 1 tbsp
orange flower water

Preheat the oven to 350°F/180°C. Sift together the flour, baking soda, cinnamon, cloves, nutmeg, and salt.

Put the oil and sugar in a bowl and beat together. Add the orange rind and juice then gradually beat in the flour mixture. Turn the mixture onto a lightly floured surface and knead for 2–3 minutes, until smooth.

Take small, egg-size pieces of dough and shape into ovals. Place on baking trays, allowing room for spreading and, with the back of a fork, press the top of each twice to make a criss-cross design. Bake the cakes in the preheated oven for about 20 minutes, until lightly browned. Transfer to a wire rack and let cool.

Meanwhile, make the topping by mixing together the walnuts and cinnamon. To make the syrup, put the honey and water in a saucepan, bring to the boil, then simmer for 5 minutes. Remove from the heat and add the lemon juice and orange juice or orange flower water.

When the cakes have almost cooled, using a slotted spoon, submerge each cake in the hot syrup and leave for about 1 minute. Place on a tray and top each with the walnut mixture. Let cool completely before serving.

Butter Cookies

easy

makes 36

prep: 15 minutes + cooling

15 minutes cooking

³/₄ cup butter

³/₄ cup superfine sugar

1 egg

2 cups self-rising flour

finely grated rind of 1 lemon

3 tbsp slivered almonds (optional)

Preheat the oven to 350°F/180°C. Put the butter and sugar in a bowl and whisk until light and fluffy. Whisk in the egg then fold in the flour and lemon rind.

Turn out the dough onto a lightly floured surface and knead gently until smooth. Form the mixture into rolls the thickness of a finger then cut into 4-inch/10-cm lengths. Shape each roll into an S shape and place on baking sheets, allowing room for spreading. If desired, stud with a few slivered almonds.

Bake the cookies in the preheated oven for about 15 minutes, until lightly browned. Cool on a wire rack. Store the cookies in an airtight tin.

Peanut Butter Cookies

Preheat the oven to 375°F/190°C. Lightly grease 2 cookie sheets with a little butter.

Beat the softened butter and peanut butter together in a large mixing bowl. Gradually add the granulated sugar and beat well. Add the beaten egg, a little at a time, beating after each addition until thoroughly blended.

Sift the flour, baking powder, and salt into the creamed peanut butter mixture.

Add the chopped peanuts and bring the mixture together with your fingers to form a soft, sticky dough. Wrap the cookie dough in plastic wrap and chill in the refrigerator for 30 minutes.

Form the dough into 20 balls and place them on the prepared cookie sheets, spaced well apart to allow room to expand during cooking, and flatten slightly with your hand.

Bake in the preheated oven for 15 minutes, until golden brown. Transfer the cookies to a wire rack and let cool before serving.

easy

makes 20

prep: 15 minutes +
cooling/chilling

15 minutes cooking

$^1/_2$ cup butter, softened, plus extra for greasing
$^1/_2$ cup chunky peanut butter
generous 1 cup granulated sugar
1 egg, beaten lightly
generous 1 cup all-purpose flour
$^1/_2$ tsp baking powder
pinch of salt
$^1/_2$ cup chopped unsalted
natural peanuts

INDEX